THE STORY OF
HELEN KELLER

A Biography Book for New Readers

—— Written by ——
Christine Platt

—— Illustrated by ——
Ana Sanfelippo

ROCKRIDGE
PRESS

In honor and celebration
of people with disabilities
everywhere!

Series Designer: Angela Navarra

Interior and Cover Designer: Scott Petrower

Art Producer: Tom Hood

Editor: Eliza Kirby

Production Editor: Ashley Polikoff

Illustration © 2020 Ana Sanfelippo; Photography Library of Congress/Alamy, pp. 46, 47, 49; Author Photo courtesy of Norman E. Jones Photography; Illustrator Photo courtesy of Miriam Herrera

ISBN: Print 978-1-64611-107-7 | eBook 978-1-64611-108-4

R0

CONTENTS

CHAPTER 1

AN INSPIRATION IS BORN

Meet Helen Keller

As a child, Helen Keller loved eating hot dogs and sweet treats. She also loved playing with her family dog, Belle, and making ice cream with her friend Martha. Helen's childhood might sound ordinary, but it wasn't. That's because something happened early in Helen's life that would make her *extraordinary*.

Helen was born on June 27, 1880, in the small town of Tuscumbia, Alabama. She was a healthy baby. But when she was just 19 months old, Helen got sick with a mysterious illness. Some historians believe it was scarlet fever. It changed her life forever.

Once she got better, Helen could no longer see or hear. This **disability** is known as being **deafblind**. In the 1800s, many people believed the deafblind couldn't learn to read and write. But today, deafblind people all around the world are educated and have wonderful lives.

Helen proved that it could be done! She overcame every challenge to become a famous **humanitarian**, educator, author, and **civil rights** leader.

WHERE?

WISCONSIN

MICHIGAN

NEW YORK

PENNSYLVANIA

NEW JERSEY

OHIO

ILLINOIS INDIANA

WEST VIRGINIA

MARYLAND

DELAWARE

MISSOURI

KENTUCKY VIRGINIA

NORTH CAROLINA

TUSCUMBIA

TENNESSEE

ARKANSAS

SOUTH CAROLINA

MISSISSIPPI ALABAMA GEORGIA

 ## Helen's America

When Helen was born, America was still recovering from the **Civil War**. The war began in 1861 and lasted four years. The southern states used **enslaved people** as free labor and wanted to keep doing so. The northern states believed **slavery** was unfair and needed to end. The northern **Union Army** defeated the southern **Confederate Army**, and the war ended on April 9, 1865. Slavery was **abolished**.

After the war, Helen's hometown of
Tuscumbia was nothing like the small thriving
town it had once been. Before, a railroad had
run through Tuscumbia, making it easy to ship
goods. But the railroad was destroyed in the war.

The Kellers had used slave labor on their
cotton **plantation**. After the war, they could not
enslave people anymore. The Kellers weren't

poor, but they weren't as wealthy as before. A formerly enslaved woman named Ms. Washington worked as the Kellers' family cook. Her daughter, Martha, would play a special role in Helen's life.

Despite Helen's illness that caused her to become deafblind, she accomplished many great things. Her determination to learn and succeed changed the way people thought about disabilities. Let's learn more about Helen and why she is often called the First Lady of Courage.

JUMP
—IN THE—
THINK
TANK

How would America be different if the South had won the Civil War?

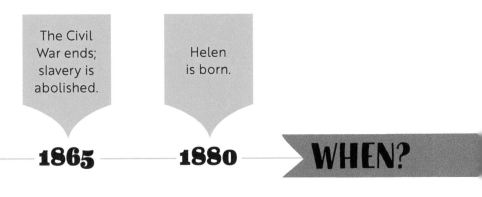

The Civil War ends; slavery is abolished.

Helen is born.

1865 — **1880** — **WHEN?**

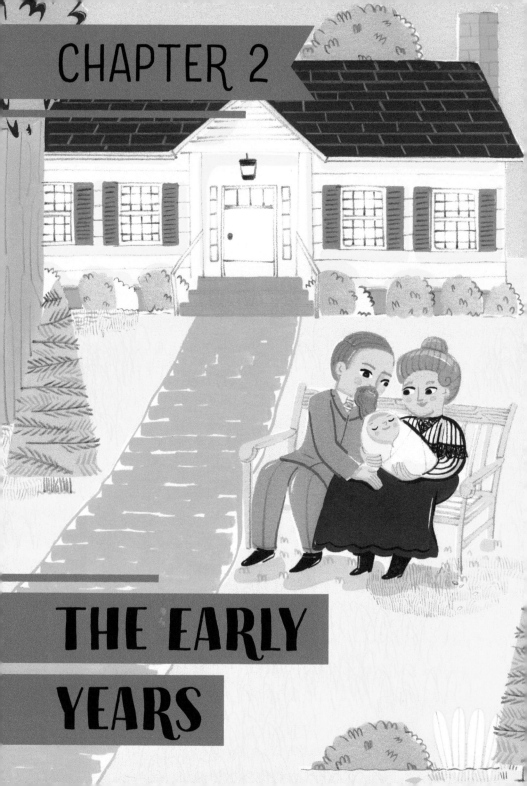

CHAPTER 2

THE EARLY
YEARS

Growing Up in Tuscumbia, Alabama

Helen's father, Captain Arthur Henley Keller, fought with the Confederate Army. After the war, he worked as an editor for the local newspaper. Her mother, Kate Adams Keller,

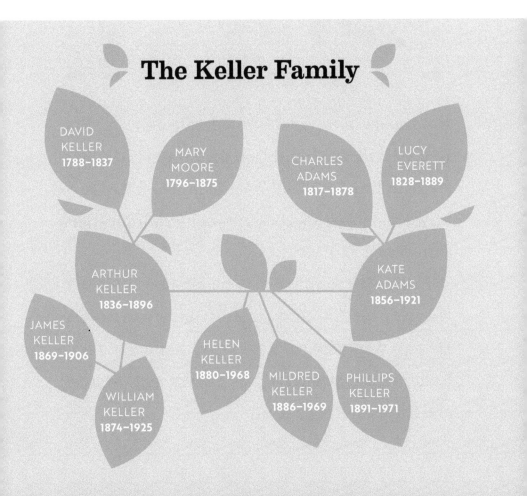

The Keller Family

DAVID KELLER
1788–1837

MARY MOORE
1796–1875

CHARLES ADAMS
1817–1878

LUCY EVERETT
1828–1889

ARTHUR KELLER
1836–1896

KATE ADAMS
1856–1921

JAMES KELLER
1869–1906

HELEN KELLER
1880–1968

MILDRED KELLER
1886–1969

PHILLIPS KELLER
1891–1971

WILLIAM KELLER
1874–1925

was the daughter of a Confederate general. The
Kellers had three children together: Helen; her
younger brother, Phillips; and her younger sister,
Mildred. Helen also had two older half brothers,
James and William.

The Keller family lived on a plantation that
Helen's grandfather had built many years before.
Helen's Aunt Evelyn lived with them, too. The
Keller family **property** was known as Ivy Green
and it was very beautiful.

Ivy Green had more than 640 acres of farmland, which is the size of about 480 football fields! There was a lot of room to grow **crops** and raise **livestock**. There was also a lot of room for the Keller children to run and play. There were plenty of trees for them to climb. Their garden had lovely flowers like roses and honeysuckles.

There was a little cottage at Ivy Green, a short walk from the main house. One day, this beautiful little cottage would become a special place for Helen.

The Fever that Changed Everything

When Helen was 19 months old, she became very sick. Her parents didn't know what to do. Even doctors

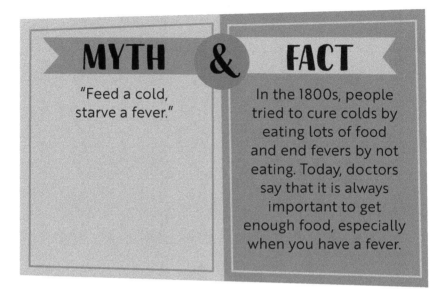

didn't know what was wrong. Their medicine didn't help Helen get better. Soon, little Helen had a dangerously high fever. Everyone was afraid she wouldn't survive.

It was a miracle Helen survived the mysterious illness. But once she got better, her parents noticed she wasn't the same playful toddler. Helen often bumped into things as though she didn't see them. They realized the fever had caused Helen to become **blind**.

Whenever anyone called out to Helen, she didn't hear them. Soon, they realized Helen was also **deaf**— she'd lost her sense of hearing. Helen was deafblind.

Because there was no cure for being deafblind, everyone felt very sorry for Helen. Her family didn't know how they would talk to her or how she would learn. But Helen would surprise everyone as she overcame the challenges of being unable to see and hear.

JUMP
—IN THE—
THINK
TANK

How do you think Helen's family felt knowing she couldn't see or hear them?

Helen is born.

Helen's fever causes her to become deafblind.

1880 — **1882** — **WHEN?**

CHAPTER 3

WILD CHILD

Making Sense of a New World

Helen had always been a very smart toddler. She could speak a few words and walk by the age of one. But Helen's new world was dark and silent. No one knew how Helen felt. Even though her family loved her, she often felt alone.

How would you communicate if you couldn't use words to express what you were thinking or feeling?

Whenever Helen got frustrated, she had temper tantrums. She never got in trouble because everyone felt sorry for her. Sometimes Helen's parents even gave her candy to calm her down! This only made her behavior worse—it was like she was getting a reward. Helen was also jealous of her baby sister, Mildred. She often had tantrums to take her parents' attention away from Mildred. By the time Helen was five years old, she was a wild, disobedient child.

Helen used her hands to let people know what she wanted. When she needed her mother, Helen put her hand on her cheek. She often played with the family cook's daughter, Martha Washington. Martha was one of the first people who understood Helen's hand **gestures**. Together, the two girls created a secret language of more than 60 hand gestures!

As Helen grew older, she used her sense of smell and touch to understand the world. For example, her father's footsteps were heavier than her mother's. Helen knew who was walking nearby by how softly or heavily the floorboards vibrated under her feet. Helen's family was grateful she discovered these things. But they really wanted doctors to help her see and hear again.

Every doctor said the same thing—Helen's sight and hearing couldn't be fixed. By the time Helen was six years old, her parents had almost given up hope.

One day, Helen's mother learned about a woman named Laura Bridgman. Like Helen, Laura became deafblind after a childhood illness. But Laura had learned to read and lived a happy life. Helen's parents decided to try one more doctor, a man named Dr. J. Julian Chisholm.

He lived in Baltimore, Maryland, which was far from Tuscumbia. They hoped Dr. Chisholm could help Helen, so they went to meet him.

Unfortunately, Dr. Chisholm couldn't help Helen.

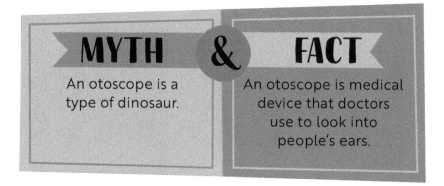

But he knew someone who could—Alexander Graham Bell. Mr. Bell was famous for inventing the telephone, but he also worked with deaf children. The Kellers met with him in Washington, DC. He knew about a special school, the Perkins Institution for the Blind. It was where Laura received her education. Mr. Bell told the Kellers to contact the school's director, Michael Anagnos. Finally, there was hope for Helen!

In their letter to Mr. Anagnos, the Kellers asked for a teacher for Helen. A few weeks later, they received wonderful news. Mr. Anagnos had found the perfect teacher—a woman named Anne Sullivan.

WHERE?

PENNSYLVANIA

BALTIMORE

OHIO

MARYLAND

DELAWARE

ILLINOIS   INDIANA

WEST VIRGINIA

WASHINGTON, DC

KENTUCKY   VIRGINIA

TENNESSEE   NORTH CAROLINA

TUSCUMBIA

SOUTH CAROLINA

MISSISSIPPI   ALABAMA   GEORGIA

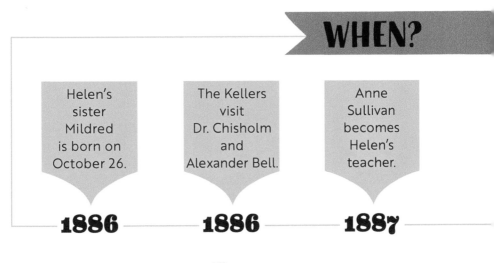

WHEN?

Helen's sister Mildred is born on October 26.	The Kellers visit Dr. Chisholm and Alexander Bell.	Anne Sullivan becomes Helen's teacher.
1886	**1886**	**1887**

CHAPTER 4

A TEACHER COMES TO STAY

The Day that Changed Helen's Life

Anne Sullivan traveled more than 1,000 miles from Boston, Massachusetts, to Tuscumbia, Alabama. When she arrived on March 3, 1887, the Kellers learned Anne also had a sight disability! She wasn't blind, but her vision was **impaired**. She could only see well enough to read if she used special glasses that were very heavy and uncomfortable.

Shortly after she arrived, Anne gave Helen a gift, a doll. She used **sign language** to spell the letters d-o-l-l in the palm of Helen's hand. Helen was very confused. She knew what a doll was. But she didn't know the word "doll." Frustrated, Helen had a tantrum. She pinched and hit Anne many times. But unlike her parents, Anne did not give Helen candy to calm her down.

For the next lesson, Anne gave Helen a mug. She **signed** m-u-g in the palm of Helen's hand.

This time, Helen was so frustrated that she broke the mug! Every time Anne tried to teach Helen, she had a tantrum. Anne didn't blame Helen. It *was* hard to learn sign language. The next morning, Helen walked around the room and ate other people's breakfast with her hands. The Kellers didn't stop her. Anne couldn't believe it! She told the Kellers the first thing Helen needed to learn was how to be obedient.

During a walk, Anne saw the beautiful little cottage on the Kellers' property. She had an idea. Because Helen's parents loved and felt

sorry for her, they kept allowing her bad behavior. Helen needed some time away from them. What if Helen could live with Anne for a short time in the cottage?

JUMP
—IN THE—
THINK TANK

Can you think of a teacher in your life who has helped you the way Anne helped Helen?

At first, Helen's parents didn't like the idea. But eventually they agreed. They took Helen on a long carriage ride to make her think she'd traveled far away. At the cottage, Anne taught Helen how to behave. She also continued their sign language lessons. It worked! Soon, Helen stopped throwing tantrums and started copying Anne's sign language.

A New Language

Even though Helen copied Anne, she didn't yet understand that things had names. She could make signs, but she didn't know what they meant. One day, Anne and Helen walked to the well.

Anne pumped water over one of Helen's hands and signed the letters w-a-t-e-r in the other. Suddenly, Helen made the connection. She was so excited! Within hours, she learned almost 30 new words.

Soon, Helen knew hundreds of words. She even tried to teach her dog sign language—but Belle preferred naps. Then Anne began teaching Helen how to read. Books for the visually impaired are printed with raised ink so readers can trace the letters with their fingers. Helen also learned how to read in **braille**—a form of writing where raised dots represent letters. Helen loved reading. She discovered

> 66 I knew then that "w-a-t-e-r" meant the wonderful cool something that was flowing over my hand. That living word awakened my soul, gave it light, hope, joy, set it free! 99

stories, myths, and facts about the world around her.

Many children (and teachers) might have given up. But Helen was determined to learn. And Anne was determined to teach her. Before she was even a teenager, Helen had achieved what many people thought was impossible. With Anne by her side, she was just getting started.

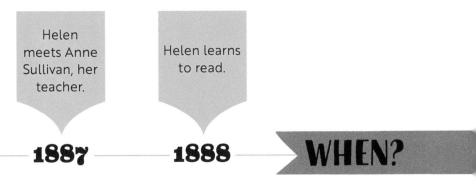

Helen meets Anne Sullivan, her teacher.

Helen learns to read.

1887 — 1888 — WHEN?

CHAPTER 5

NEW

DREAMS

Learning to Speak

Newspapers began publishing stories about Anne and Helen. Even President Grover Cleveland wanted to meet the amazing Helen Keller. Along with Anne, Helen visited the White House before she was 10 years old. She would meet more than a dozen presidents in her life!

Visiting the White House was great. But there was one place Helen really wanted to go—the Perkins Institution for the Blind in Boston, Massachusetts. Both Laura and Anne went to school there, and Helen wanted to do the same.

In 1888, Helen and Anne traveled to Boston. Anne had become more than Helen's teacher. She was her guardian and most trusted friend. Together, they explored Boston. The large city was different from Tuscumbia. Helen enjoyed taking in the new smells and eating Northern food.

Helen felt like she'd finally found her place in the world at Perkins. Everyone there was just like her. Helen and her new friends used sign language to communicate. They also read books in braille.

> ❝ I was **delighted** to find that nearly all of my **new friends** could spell with their fingers. Oh, what happiness! ❞

Helen studied many subjects at Perkins. English was one of her favorite classes, especially when they read poetry. Helen discovered she also loved to write, and she often created her own stories and poems.

In March 1890, Helen learned about a deafblind girl who lived in Norway. This girl had learned to speak. Helen couldn't believe it! She knew her family spoke with their mouths. It was one of the reasons she had tantrums as a child—she wanted to speak to them. And if another deafblind girl had learned to speak, Helen was determined to do the same.

At first, Anne didn't think it was good idea. Helen couldn't *hear* words, so how could she learn to *speak*? Helen's goal seemed impossible, but she refused to take no for an answer. Finally, Anne agreed—she would try to teach Helen how to talk.

The Horace Mann School for the Deaf and Hard of Hearing was also in Boston. Anne took Helen to meet the principal, Sarah Fuller. Ms. Fuller offered to help Helen. Ms. Fuller placed Helen's fingers on her lips and throat. When Ms. Fuller

JUMP -IN THE- THINK TANK

Have you ever heard about someone just like you who did something that seemed impossible? Were you inspired by them?

spoke, Helen could feel the vibrations of each word! After 11 lessons with Ms. Fuller, Anne continued to teach Helen.

Learning speech was hard. Helen often became frustrated, but thanks to Anne, she had grown out of her tantrums. Helen continued to practice. Soon, she could make her first sounds. Then, when she was 10, Helen spoke her first sentence: "It is too warm." She had set a huge goal for herself—and she had reached it!

In 1894, Anne took Helen to New York City
to attend the Wright-Humason School for the
Deaf. Helen was the only student there who was
deafblind. In class, Anne read the assignment

and signed the words into Helen's hands. Meanwhile, Helen continued learning to speak.

Helen was 13 years old. Like most teenagers, she wanted to explore New York. Helen learned much about the city through her sense of smell and touch. Although she had fun, Helen found it too busy.

When Helen finished her schooling at Wright-Humason, she set her next goal. She wanted to attend college! But during this time, some people thought women shouldn't go to college. College seemed impossible for a woman who was also deafblind. Helen's mother thought she was too young. Even Anne agreed. But once Helen set her mind to something, she couldn't be stopped.

Helen's mother agreed under one condition—Helen had to go to boarding school to get ready for college. In 1896, Helen enrolled in the Cambridge School for Young Ladies. There, she studied for her college entrance exams.

Helen wanted to go to Harvard University. At the time only men were allowed, so Helen applied to Harvard's school for women, Radcliffe College. She was nervous waiting to find out if she'd gotten in. Then one day a letter arrived from Radcliffe College—Helen was accepted! She couldn't wait to begin.

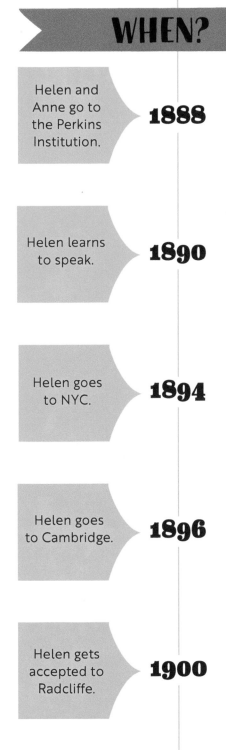

WHEN?

Helen and Anne go to the Perkins Institution. **1888**

Helen learns to speak. **1890**

Helen goes to NYC. **1894**

Helen goes to Cambridge. **1896**

Helen gets accepted to Radcliffe. **1900**

CHAPTER 6

HIGHER EDUCATION

Going to Radcliffe

Radcliffe College was just outside of Boston. Unlike the other schools that Helen had attended, her classmates at Radcliffe could hear and see. None of Helen's textbooks were available in braille, so Anne read and **translated** them. She also attended classes with Helen and translated the professor's **lectures**.

College classes weren't easy. They were extra hard for Helen because she was deafblind. Most other students could review their textbooks and class notes, but Helen had to memorize everything. She had to work so much harder in order to succeed. Of course, Helen did just that. She got excellent grades, even outsmarting some of her classmates.

66 It is so **pleasant** to learn about **new things. 99**

A Love of Writing

Helen had loved studying English in grade school, and she still enjoyed English classes in college. Mr. Charles Copeland taught English at Radcliffe. He thought Helen's writing was fantastic. Mr. Copeland encouraged Helen

to write more, especially about her experiences as a deafblind person.

Helen used a **typewriter** to write. She memorized the location of each letter. They had the same placement as the letters on today's keyboards and laptops.

Many people were surprised that Helen could type faster than people who could see!

Helen had always enjoyed writing stories and poetry. With the encouragement of Mr. Copeland, she began to write more about her life and experiences as a deafblind woman. Some of Helen's stories and articles were published. In 1903, Helen wrote her first book, *The Story of My Life*. The **autobiography** followed the journey of Helen's life, from childhood through becoming a student at Radcliffe. Of course, Helen spoke throughout the book of her love and appreciation for Anne.

The book was very successful. It is still read by people all over the world. *The Story of My Life* was the first book Helen wrote, but it wouldn't be the last. Helen would write a dozen books.

JUMP
—IN THE—
THINK
TANK

Have you ever wanted to write the story of your life? What would you say about yourself and the life you've lived?

As people read *The Story of My Life*, Helen became more famous. Everyone from doctors to world leaders wanted to meet her. She even made friends with a famous writer, Mark Twain. Helen's classmates admired her, too. In 1902,

they gave her a special gift. After learning that one of Helen's beloved dogs had passed away, her classmates gave her a new pet, a Boston Terrier named Sir Thomas.

Despite her growing fame, Helen continued to study at Radcliffe. In 1904, Helen did something no deafblind person had ever done—she graduated from college. Not only was Helen the first deafblind person to earn a college degree, she also graduated with high honors. This success wasn't the last of Helen's achievements. She still had more great things to do.

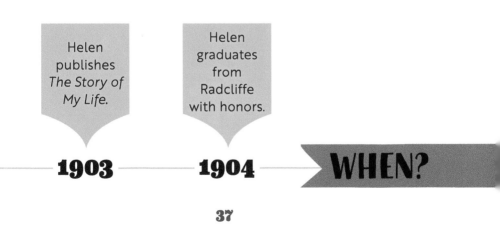

Helen publishes *The Story of My Life.*

Helen graduates from Radcliffe with honors.

1903 — 1904 — **WHEN?**

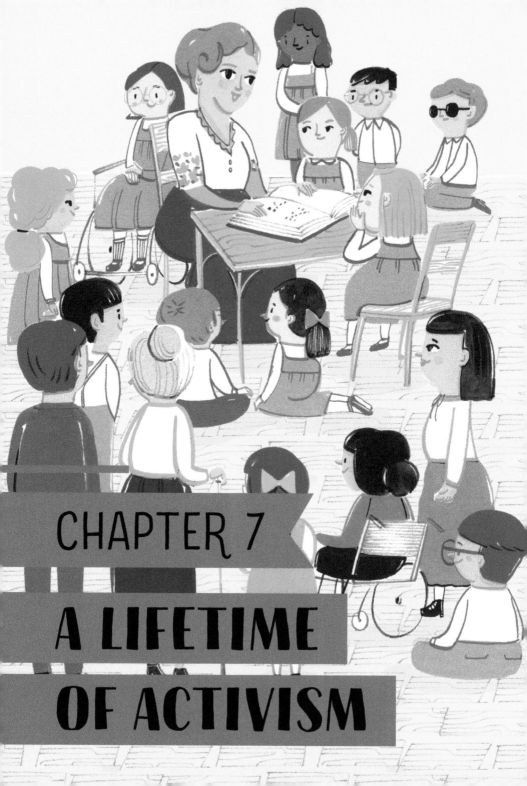

CHAPTER 7

A LIFETIME OF ACTIVISM

Touring the World

After graduating from Radcliffe, Helen's work wasn't done. She knew she'd accomplished so much because she was **privileged**. Helen's parents were wealthy, so they could hire Anne as her teacher. But Helen believed everyone deserved the right to an education. She became an **activist** dedicated to helping people with disabilities.

Helen often traveled to share her life story. She explained that people with disabilities could learn if given the right opportunities. She also helped people with disabilities she met at her lectures, offering them encouragement and guidance.

By the early 1900s, Helen was a well-known **advocate** for people with disabilities. She even **testified** before **Congress**, which is responsible for governing the nation. Helen told Congress that it was important to improve the lives of blind people. A year later, the president signed a new law that helped give books in braille to people who needed them.

In 1915, Helen created her own organization, Helen Keller International. She worked with a man named George Kessler, a very successful businessman. Together they tried to end some of the causes of blindness, such as **malnutrition**. Then, in 1920, Helen helped create one of America's most important organizations, the American Civil Liberties Union (ACLU). More than 100 years later, the ACLU continues to protect the rights of every American.

66 If I, deaf, blind, find life rich and interesting, how much more can you gain by the use of your five senses! 99

40

Helen continued to travel and speak out about her views, even when others disagreed. For example, she advocated for women having the right to vote. Anne continued to support and encourage her.

In 1936, Anne became very ill. When she passed away on October 20, Helen was there holding her hand. They'd been nearly inseparable for almost 50 years. Of course, Helen was devastated by Anne's death. She felt very lonely. But she knew Anne would have wanted her to continue her important work.

Sharing Her Story and Advocating for Others

Helen had many roles in her lifetime, but one of the biggest came in 1946. Helen became counselor on international relations for the American Foundation for Overseas Blind. For the next 10 years, she traveled to 35 countries to help raise awareness about blindness. One of those trips included a 40,000-mile, five-month tour across Asia—when Helen was 75 years old!

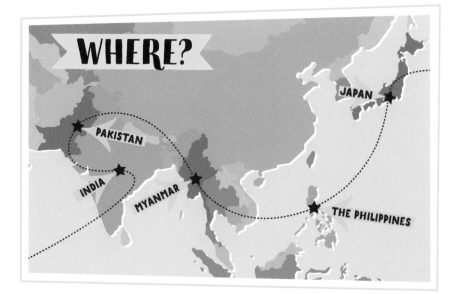

WHERE?

JAPAN

PAKISTAN

INDIA

MYANMAR

THE PHILIPPINES

Helen received many honors. In 1936, she received the Theodore Roosevelt Distinguished Service Medal. In 1964, she received the Presidential Medal of Freedom. In 1961, Helen became ill and began to spend more time at her home in Connecticut. In 1965, she was elected to the National Women's Hall of Fame. When Helen passed away on June 1, 1968, she was buried at a special memorial at the National Cathedral in Washington, DC—right next to her teacher and best friend, Anne Sullivan.

Helen's life continues to serve as an inspiration for overcoming challenges to achieve great things. Helen's determination changed not only her own life, but also the lives of millions of people with disabilities. She forever changed the world we live in today by advocating for **equality** for everyone. Helen Keller remains one of the most celebrated women in history.

WHEN?

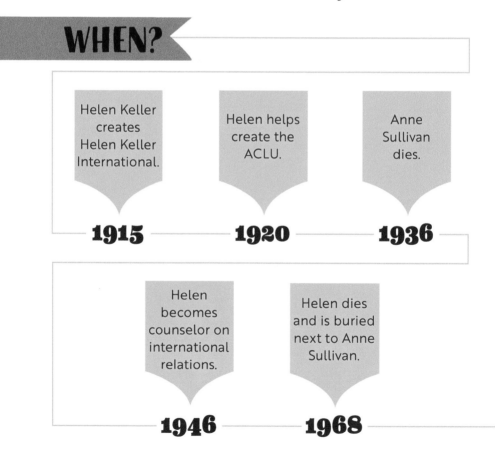

Helen Keller creates Helen Keller International.

Helen helps create the ACLU.

Anne Sullivan dies.

1915 — **1920** — **1936**

Helen becomes counselor on international relations.

Helen dies and is buried next to Anne Sullivan.

1946 — **1968**

CHAPTER 8

SO . . . WHO WAS HELEN KELLER

?

Challenge Accepted!

Now that you have learned how Helen Keller's determination and activism changed the world, let's test your new knowledge in a little who, what, when, where, why, and how quiz. Feel free to look back in the text to find the answers if you need to, but try to remember first!

1 **Where was Helen born?**

→ A   Montgomery, Alabama

→ B   Tuscumbia, Alabama

→ C   Washington, DC

→ D   Boston, Massachusetts

2 **How old was Helen when she became deafblind?**

→ A   Nineteen months old

→ B   Five years old

→ C   Ten years old

→ D   Helen was born deafblind

3 **Who was the teacher who helped Helen learn sign language?**

 A Anne Brown

→ B Anne Keller

→ C Anne Sullivan

→ D Anne Bell

4 **What was the name of the first school that Helen attended?**

→ A Helen never attend school

→ B The Perkins Institution for the Blind

→ C Radcliffe College

→ D Wright-Humason School for the Deaf

5 **How did Helen learn to communicate?**

→ A Using sign language

→ B Using a typewriter

→ C Through speaking

→ D All of the above

6 How many presidents did Helen meet in her lifetime?

→ A One

→ B Three

→ C Five

→ D More than ten

7 What was Helen's favorite subject?

→ A English, especially poetry

→ B Math, especially algebra

→ C Science, especially chemistry

→ D Helen didn't really like school

8 What was the name of Helen's first book?

→ A *I Am Helen Keller*

→ B *It's Me, Helen Keller*

→ C *The Story of My Life*

→ D *The Helen Keller Story*

9 When Helen was 75 years old, she made a 40,000-mile, five-month tour across which continent?

→ A   Asia

→ B   Africa

→ C   Antarctica

→ D   Australia

10 Which awards and honors did Helen receive?

→ A   Theodore Roosevelt Distinguished Service Medal

→ B   Presidential Medal of Freedom

→ C   Women's Hall of Fame

→ D   All of the above

Our World

The benefits of Helen's work can still be seen today:

→ People with disabilities are able to receive an education and attend college.

→ More people understand and respect people with disabilities and are dedicated to making opportunities accessible to everyone.

→ The ACLU continues to protect the constitutional rights of every American.

JUMP
—IN THE—
THINK
TANK
FOR

⁓ MORE! ⁓

Now let's think a little more about what Helen Keller did, and how her actions and determination affected our world.

→ By overcoming her challenges, Helen was able to prove that people with disabilities could achieve great things. What are some challenges that you can overcome to prove people wrong?

→ Helen was determined to achieve her goals. What are some goals that you are determined to achieve, no matter how impossible they might seem?

→ What are some ways that you can continue Helen's work for equal rights and opportunities for everyone?

Glossary

abolished: Put an end to something, such as a law, policy, or practice like slavery

activist: A person who takes action for or against a side of an issue

advocate: A person who defends or supports a cause or person

autobiography: The story of a person's life written by that person

blind: Unable to see

braille: A written language for blind people that uses patterns of raised dots that are felt (read) with the fingertips

civil rights: The rights that are granted to every citizen to be treated fairly and equally

Civil War: A war between the southern Confederate Army and northern Union Army of the United States that ended slavery

Confederate Army: The army of soldiers from the southern states who wanted to keep slavery legal

Congress: Part of the United States government made up of representatives from different parts of the country

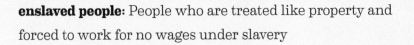

crops: Plants that are farmed to be used as food, such as grains, fruits, and vegetables

deaf: Unable to hear

deafblind: Unable to hear and see

disability: A physical or mental condition that limits a person's movements, senses, or activities

enslaved people: People who are treated like property and forced to work for no wages under slavery

equality: Being equal; when every person in a group has the same rights and opportunities

gesture: A movement of part of the body to express an idea or meaning, often with one's hands

humanitarian: A person who works to help everyone have better lives; a person who works to help stop others from suffering

impaired: Having a disability of a specified kind such as hearing or vision loss

lecture: An educational talk to an audience

livestock: Farm animals such as cows, pigs, sheep, goats, and horses

malnutrition: Lack of proper nutrition, often caused by not having enough to eat or not eating enough healthy food

plantation: An estate that uses manual labor to take care of crops and agriculture such as cotton, tobacco, and sugar

privileged: Having special rights or opportunities only granted to certain people instead of everyone

property: A thing or things belonging to someone

sign language: A system of communication that uses signs, gestures, body language, and facial expression

signed: The use of hand gestures to communicate

slavery: A labor system in which people are treated like property and forced to work for no wages

testify: Giving evidence or information to help prove something, especially in a legal case

translated: The act of changing one language into another

typewriter: A machine with keys for producing alphabetical characters, numerals, and symbols one at a time on paper

Union Army: The army of soldiers from the northern states who wanted slavery to be abolished

Bibliography

Einhorn, Lois J. *Helen Keller, Public Speakers: Sightless but Seen, Deaf but Heard*. Greenwood Press, 1998.

Ford, Cain. *Helen Keller: Lighting the Way for the Blind and Deaf*. Enslow Publishers, 2001.

"Helen Keller." American Foundation for the Blind. 2020.

"Helen Keller." The Perkins School for the Blind. 2020.

Hermann, Dorothy. *Helen Keller: A Life*. University of Chicago Press, 1998.

Keller, Helen. *The Story of My Life*. 1903.

Keller, Helen. *The World I Live In*. 1910.

Lash, Joseph. *Helen and Teacher: The Story of Helen Keller and Anne Sullivan Macy*. Delacorte Press, 1980.

Michals, Debra. "Helen Keller." National Women's History Museum. 2020.

Weatherford, Doris. *American Women's History: An A to Z of People, Organizations, Issues, and Events*. Prentice Hall, 1994.

Acknowledgments

I would like to acknowledge and honor the Perkins School for the Blind, the American Foundation for the Blind, and Helen Keller International for their continued efforts as champions and advocates for the deafblind community.

About the Author

CHRISTINE PLATT is a literacy advocate and passionate activist for social justice and policy reform. She holds a BA in Africana studies from the University of South Florida, an MA in African and African American studies from The Ohio State University, and a JD from Stetson University College of Law. A believer in the power of storytelling as a tool for social change, Christine's literature centers on teaching race, equity, diversity, and inclusion to people of all ages.

About the Illustrator

ANA SANFELIPPO is from Buenos Aires, Argentina. Her work includes illustrations for books, magazines, patterns, and products. She has published many children's books and has shown her work at exhibitions in Argentina, Slovakia, England, Canada, and Spain. She combines many hand-drawn techniques, and loves creating natural sceneries and funny characters with many vibrant colors.

WHO WILL INSPIRE YOU NEXT?

EXPLORE A WORLD OF HEROES AND ROLE MODELS IN
***THE STORY OF*...** BIOGRAPHY SERIES FOR NEW READERS.

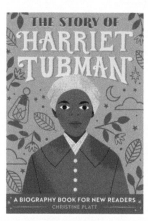

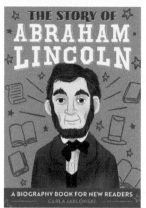

LOOK FOR THIS SERIES
WHEREVER BOOKS AND EBOOKS ARE SOLD

Alexander Hamilton

Albert Einstein

Martin Luther King Jr.

George Washington

Jane Goodall

Barack Obama

The Wright Brothers

Marie Curie